May He who sends the raindrops
And makes the sunshine, too,
Look down and bless you richly
And be very near to you!

Helen Steiner Rice

*Thou hast fixed all the bounds of the earth; thou*
*hast made summer and winter.*
*Psalm 74:17*

*So we may know God better*
*And feel His quiet power,*
*Let us daily keep in silence*
*A meditation hour.*

December 31, 1997 (Wednesday)

Tonight I attended new Year's Eve service at Oak Grove A.M.E. Church. This is my Church. Rev. Gregory and Rev. Jessica delivered the message entitled "Coming Out." It was delivered in two parts. Rev. Jessica first, Rev. Gregory second, and Rev. Jessica finishing up. They were dynamic together. The mass choir sang and I believe were truly annointed with Praise. Two of the songs we sang were "Total Praise" (one of my favorites) and "Love Holiday" which is quickly becoming (I should say already has) become one of my favorites. Thank God for an annointed and blessed service.

**M**ay the words of my mouth and the meditation of my heart
be pleasing in your sight, O Lord, my Rock and my Redeemer.
Psalm 19:15 NIV

## January 1, 1998 (Thursday)

Today is New Year's Day and I thank God for allowing me to see another new year, this year of Our Lord 1998. Thank You Lord for allowing me to be in the house of the Lord when the new year came in.

Today is going to be quiet day for me. A day of reflecting. Thinking about what I want to accomplish in 1998. What my life is going to be like in 1998. I am making two (2) resolutions this year. One, to faithfully keep a journal this year and two to really seek what God wants me to do in my life. Asking Him to show me what He would have me do and for my obedience in what He shows me.

I wrapped 5-6 books for Come Home for Christmas. Glad I did them today

*I sometimes think that friendliness*
*Is like a cheerful song ...*
*It makes the good days better,*
*And it helps when things go wrong.*

## January 2, 1998 (Friday)

Well, I thought I had finished wrapping for "Gone Home For Christmas" but Denise Glover's mom is sick and she is at home with her, so I'll finish them today. Rev. Mamie Rowe, her daughter and another lady I did not know brought the remaining books to be wrapped and picked up the ones I had wrapped. It is about 1:00 A.M on Saturday morning and I have finished wrapping the remainder of the books with totaled thirty eight (38). Denise Glover and I wrapped some on Tuesday Dec. 30. They are now all done. I think Denise said you had a total of 170. On Tuesday Dorothy and I went to Northland to get a couple of things she wanted and I had to wait for Denise to get the books to the church (after the funeral of Mr. Graham)

*The Lord is my strength and my shield; in him my heart trusts; so I am helped, and my heart exalts, and with my song I give thanks to him.*
*Psalm 28:7*

## January 3, 1998 (Saturday)

Today was quiet. It didn't seem to me as though I accomplished very much early in the day, but tonight I went to the dinner for the Disciples. It was a very pleasant experience. It was a blessed evening. The amount of money raised thus far was reported at ninety thousand ($90,000.00) plus. (There are still monies out to be reported) It truly was a blessing and credit to the Disciples to raise that kind of money. Truly it was all used for good causes. So many people were made happy. The food was good. It was catered by the school that Julia Parkett is principal of. Can't think of the name right now.

I prayed with Mrs Blake tonight as I do every night.

*Wait with a heart that is patient
For the goodness of God to prevail,
For never do our prayers go unanswered
And His mercy and love never fail.*

January 4, 1998 (Sunday)

Thank You, God for waking me this morning with a mind to go to your Sanctuary to praise and worship you. God you are worthy to be praised.

*Rest in the Lord and wait patiently for Him.*
*Psalm 37:7 NAS*

There's something we should not forget —
That people we've known or heard of or met
By indirection have a big part
In molding the thoughts of the mind and the heart.

_____

_____

_____

_____

_____

_____

_____

_____

_____

_____

_____

_____

_____

_____

_____

_____

_____

_____

_____

_____

_____

_____

*A man's heart deviseth his way:
but the Lord directeth his steps.
Proverbs 16:9 KJV*

Among the great and glorious gifts
Our heavenly Father sends
Is the gift of understanding
That we find in loving friends.

*A* friend loves at all times, and a brother is born for adversity.
Proverbs 17:17

*Great is your gladness*
*And rich your reward*
*When you make life's purpose*
*The choice of the Lord.*

---

*Happiness is something*
*We create in our mind,*
*It's something you search for*
*And so seldom find.*

_____

_____
_____
_____
_____
_____
_____
_____
_____
_____
_____
_____
_____
_____
_____
_____
_____
_____
_____
_____
_____
_____
_____
_____
_____
_____
_____
_____

*You shall eat the fruit of the labour of your hands;*
*you shall be happy, and it shall be well with you.*
*Psalm 128:2*

*Every home*
*Is specially blessed*
*When God becomes*
*A daily guest.*

_____

_____
_____
_____
_____
_____
_____
_____
_____
_____
_____
_____
_____
_____
_____
_____
_____
_____
_____
_____
_____
_____
_____
_____
_____
_____

*Every day I will bless thee, and praise thy name for ever and ever.*
*Psalm 145:2*

May He who hears each little prayer
Keep you safely in His care
And make the world around you bright
As you walk daily in His light.

*Thy word is a lamp to my feet and a light to my path.*
*Psalm 119:105*

No matter how big man's dreams are,
God's blessings are infinitely more,
For always God's giving is greater
Than what man is asking for.

*He* will receive blessing from the Lord, and
vindication from the God of his salvation.
Psalm 24:5

Dear God, what a comfort
To know that You care
And to know when I seek You,
You will always be there!

*He keeps you from all evil, and preserves your life. He keeps his eye
upon you as you come and go, and always guards you.
Psalm 121:7, 8 TLB*

*Kneel in prayer in His presence,*
*And you'll find no need to speak.*
*For softly in silent communion,*
*God grants you the peace that you seek.*

---

*For God alone my soul waits in silence; from him comes my salvation.*
*Psalm 62:1*

As you climb life's ladder,
Take faith along with you,
And great will be your happiness
As your dearest dreams come true.

_Love the Lord, all you his saints! The Lord preserves the
faithful, but abundantly requites him who acts haughtily._
Psalm 31:23

*Grant me faith and courage,*
*Put purpose in my days,*
*Show me how to serve Thee*
*In the most effective ways.*

_____

_____

_____

_____

_____

_____

_____

_____

_____

_____

_____

_____

_____

_____

_____

_____

_____

_____

_____

_____

_____

_____

_____

_____

_____

_____

_____

*Wait on the Lord: be of good courage, and he shall*
*strengthen thine heart: wait, I say, on the Lord.*
*Psalm 27:14 KJV*

We are all God's children,
And He loves us — every one,
And completely forgives
All that we have done.

_____
_____
_____
_____
_____
_____
_____
_____
_____
_____
_____
_____
_____
_____
_____
_____
_____
_____
_____
_____
_____
_____
_____
_____

*T*rain up a child in the way he should go,
even when he is old he will not depart from it.
Proverbs 22:6 NAS

By completing what God
Gives us to do,
We find real contentment
And happiness, too.

*God* blesses those who obey him; happy the
man who puts his trust in the Lord.
*Proverbs 16:20 TLB*

To understand God's greatness
And to use His gifts each day
The soul must learn to meet Him
In a meditative way.

_____

_____

_____

_____

_____

_____

_____

_____

_____

_____

_____

_____

_____

_____

_____

_____

_____

_____

_____

_____

_____

_____

_____

_____

*To get wisdom is better than gold; to get
understanding is to be chosen rather than silver.
Proverbs 16:16*

*We awaken in the morning,*
*Wondering how we'll meet the day,*
*Not knowing God stands ready*
*To help us if we pray.*

_____
_____
_____
_____
_____
_____
_____
_____
_____
_____
_____
_____
_____
_____
_____
_____
_____
_____
_____
_____
_____
_____
_____
_____
_____

*The integrity of the upright guides them, but the*
*crookedness of the treacherous destroys them.*
*Proverbs 11:3*

The love of God surrounds us
Like the air we breathe around us —
As near as a heartbeat, as close as a prayer,
And whenever we need Him, He'll always be there.

_____

_____

_____

_____

_____

_____

_____

_____

_____

_____

_____

_____

_____

_____

_____

_____

_____

_____

_____

_____

_____

_____

*The Lord is faithful in all his words, and gracious in all his deeds.*
*Psalm 145:13*

*Just like the seasons that come and go*
*When the flowers of spring lay buried in snow,*
*God sends to the heart in its winter of sadness*
*A springtime awakening of new hope and gladness.*

_____
_____
_____
_____
_____
_____
_____
_____
_____
_____
_____
_____
_____
_____
_____
_____
_____
_____
_____
_____
_____
_____
_____
_____
_____
_____

*And now, Lord, for what do I wait? My hope is in thee.*
*Psalm 39:7*

Deal only with the present,
Never step into tomorrow,
For God asks us just to trust Him
And to never borrow sorrow.

*For our heart rejoices in Him, because we trust in His holy name.*
*Psalm 33:21 NAS*

*When the door to our heart*
*Is open wide,*
*The sunshine of love*
*Will come inside.*

---

*Probe me, O God, and know my heart; try me and know my thoughts!*
*Psalm 139:23 NAB*

*You'll find when you smile
Your day will be brighter,
And all of your burdens
Will seem so much lighter.*

_I sought the Lord, and He answered me, and delivered
me from all my fears. Look to him, and be radiant.
Psalm 34:4, 5_

Faith is the key to heaven,
And only God's children hold
The key that opens the gateway
To that beautiful city of gold.

*This is the gate of the Lord; the righteous shall enter through it.*
Psalm 118:20

*True communication*
*Is reached through God alone,*
*To Him the thoughts we cannot express*
*Are understood and known.*

---

***How*** *precious to me are thy thoughts, O God!*
*How vast is the sum of them!*
*Psalm 139:17*

*"Love divine, all loves excelling"*
*Makes my humbled heart Your dwelling,*
*For without Your love divine*
*Total darkness would be mine.*

_____

_____

_____

_____

_____

_____

_____

_____

_____

_____

_____

_____

_____

_____

_____

_____

_____

_____

_____

_____

_____

_____

_____

_____

_____

_____

_____

*He who dwells in the shelter of the Most High, who abides in the sha-*
*dow of the Almighty, will say to the Lord, "My refuge and my fortress ..."*
*Psalm 91:1 and 2*

Faith is a force that is greater
Than knowledge or power or skill,
And the darkest defeat turns to triumph
If we trust in God's wisdom and will.

---

***T**rust in the Lord, and do good; so you will dwell in the land, and enjoy security ... Commit your way to the Lord; trust in him, and he will act.*
*Psalm 37:3, 5*

Spring always comes with new life and birth
Followed by summer to warm the soft earth —
And what a comfort to know there are reasons
That souls, like nature, must have their seasons.

The nature of our attitude
Toward circumstantial things
Determines our acceptance
Of the problems that life brings.

*But I have calmed and quieted my soul, like a child quieted at its mother's breast; like a child that is quieted is my soul.*
Psalm 131:2

*Love one another*
*And help those in need,*
*Regardless of colour,*
*Race, church, or creed.*

_____

_____
_____
_____
_____
_____
_____
_____
_____
_____
_____
_____
_____
_____
_____
_____
_____
_____
_____
_____
_____
_____
_____
_____
_____
_____
_____

*Hatred stirs old quarrels, but love overlooks insults.*
*Proverbs 10:12 TLB*

So we may know God better
And feel His quiet power,
Let us daily keep in silence
A meditation hour.

_____
_____
_____
_____
_____
_____
_____
_____
_____
_____
_____
_____
_____
_____
_____
_____
_____
_____
_____
_____
_____
_____

*May the words of my mouth and the meditation of my heart
be pleasing in your sight, O Lord, my Rock and my Redeemer.
Psalm 19:15 NIV*

*A cheerful smile, a friendly word,*
*A sympathetic nod ...*
*These are all priceless treasures*
*From the storehouse of our God.*

---

*To make an apt answer is a joy to a man,*
*and a word in season, how good it is!*
*Proverbs 15:23*

*I sometimes think that friendliness*
*Is like a cheerful song ...*
*It makes the good days better,*
*And it helps when things go wrong.*

*The Lord is my strength and my shield; in him my heart trusts; so I am helped, and my heart exalts, and with my song I give thanks to him.*
*Psalm 28:7*

*Do not sit and idly wish for wider, new dimensions*
*Where you can put in practice all your good intentions,*
*But at the spot God placed you, begin at once to do*
*Little things to brighten up the lives surrounding you.*

*The path of the righteous is like the light of dawn,*
*which shines brighter and brighter until full day.*
*Proverbs 4:18*

*Wait with a heart that is patient*
*For the goodness of God to prevail,*
*For never do our prayers go unanswered*
*And His mercy and love never fail.*

*Rest in the Lord and wait patiently for Him.*
*Psalm 37:7 NAS*

There's something we should not forget —
That people we've known or heard of or met
By indirection have a big part
In molding the thoughts of the mind and the heart.

_____

_____
_____
_____
_____
_____
_____
_____
_____
_____
_____
_____
_____
_____
_____
_____
_____
_____
_____
_____
_____
_____
_____
_____

*A man's heart deviseth his way:*
*but the Lord directeth his steps.*
*Proverbs 16:9 KJV*

*Among the great and glorious gifts*
*Our heavenly Father sends*
*Is the gift of understanding*
*That we find in loving friends.*

**A** *friend loves at all times, and a brother is born for adversity.*
*Proverbs 17:17*

*Great is your gladness*
*And rich your reward*
*When you make life's purpose*
*The choice of the Lord.*

_____
_____
_____
_____
_____
_____
_____
_____
_____
_____
_____
_____
_____
_____
_____
_____
_____
_____
_____
_____
_____
_____
_____
_____
_____
_____

*The reward for humility and fear of the*
*Lord is riches and honour and life.*
*Proverbs 22:4*

Happiness is something
We create in our mind,
It's something you search for
And so seldom find.

_____
_____
_____
_____
_____
_____
_____
_____
_____
_____
_____
_____
_____
_____
_____
_____
_____
_____
_____
_____
_____
_____
_____
_____

*You shall eat the fruit of the labour of your hands;*
*you shall be happy, and it shall be well with you.*
*Psalm 128:2*

Every home
Is specially blessed
When God becomes
A daily guest.

Every day I will bless thee, and praise thy name for ever and ever.
Psalm 145:2

May He who hears each little prayer
Keep you safely in His care
And make the world around you bright
As you walk daily in His light.

_Thy word is a lamp to my feet and a light to my path._
Psalm 119:105

*No matter how big man's dreams are,*
*God's blessings are infinitely more,*
*For always God's giving is greater*
*Than what man is asking for.*

Dear God, what a comfort
To know that You care
And to know when I seek You,
You will always be there!

_____
_____
_____
_____
_____
_____
_____
_____
_____
_____
_____
_____
_____
_____
_____
_____
_____
_____
_____
_____
_____
_____
_____
_____

*He keeps you from all evil, and preserves your life. He keeps his eye
upon you as you come and go, and always guards you.*
*Psalm 121:7, 8 TLB*

Kneel in prayer in His presence,
And you'll find no need to speak.
For softly in silent communion,
God grants you the peace that you seek.

_____

_____
_____
_____
_____
_____
_____
_____
_____
_____
_____
_____
_____
_____
_____
_____
_____
_____
_____
_____
_____
_____
_____
_____
_____
_____

*For God alone my soul waits in silence; from him comes my salvation.*
*Psalm 62:1*

As you climb life's ladder,
Take faith along with you,
And great will be your happiness
As your dearest dreams come true.

_Love the Lord, all you his saints! The Lord preserves the faithful, but abundantly requites him who acts haughtily._
Psalm 31:23

Grant me faith and courage,
Put purpose in my days,
Show me how to serve Thee
In the most effective ways.

_____
_____
_____
_____
_____
_____
_____
_____
_____
_____
_____
_____
_____
_____
_____
_____
_____
_____
_____
_____
_____
_____
_____
_____

*Wait on the Lord: be of good courage, and he shall
strengthen thine heart: wait, I say, on the Lord.*
*Psalm 27:14 KJV*

We are all God's children,
And He loves us — every one,
And completely forgives
All that we have done.

_____

_____
_____
_____
_____
_____
_____
_____
_____
_____
_____
_____
_____
_____
_____
_____
_____
_____
_____
_____
_____
_____
_____
_____

*Train up a child in the way he should go,
even when he is old he will not depart from it.
Proverbs 22:6 NAS*

*By completing what God
Gives us to do,
We find real contentment
And happiness, too.*

_____

_____
_____
_____
_____
_____
_____
_____
_____
_____
_____
_____
_____
_____
_____
_____
_____
_____
_____
_____
_____
_____
_____

*God blesses those who obey him; happy the
man who puts his trust in the Lord.
Proverbs 16:20 TLB*

To understand God's greatness
And to use His gifts each day
The soul must learn to meet Him
In a meditative way.

_____

_____

_____

_____

_____

_____

_____

_____

_____

_____

_____

_____

_____

_____

_____

_____

_____

_____

_____

_____

_____

_____

*To get wisdom is better than gold; to get*
*understanding is to be chosen rather than silver.*
Proverbs 16:16

*We awaken in the morning,*
*Wondering how we'll meet the day,*
*Not knowing God stands ready*
*To help us if we pray.*

_____
_____
_____
_____
_____
_____
_____
_____
_____
_____
_____
_____
_____
_____
_____
_____
_____
_____
_____
_____
_____
_____
_____
_____
_____

*The integrity of the upright guides them, but the*
*crookedness of the treacherous destroys them.*
*Proverbs 11:3*

The love of God surrounds us
Like the air we breathe around us —
As near as a heartbeat, as close as a prayer,
And whenever we need Him, He'll always be there.

_The Lord is faithful in all his words, and gracious in all his deeds._
_Psalm 145:13_

*Just like the seasons that come and go*
*When the flowers of spring lay buried in snow,*
*God sends to the heart in its winter of sadness*
*A springtime awakening of new hope and gladness.*

_____

_____

_____

_____

_____

_____

_____

_____

_____

_____

_____

_____

_____

_____

_____

_____

_____

_____

_____

_____

_____

_____

_____

_____

_____

*And now, Lord, for what do I wait? My hope is in thee.*
*Psalm 39:7*

Deal only with the present,
Never step into tomorrow,
For God asks us just to trust Him
And to never borrow sorrow.

*For our heart rejoices in Him, because we trust in His holy name.*
*Psalm 33:21 NAS*

*When the door to our heart*
*Is open wide,*
*The sunshine of love*
*Will come inside.*

_____
_____
_____
_____
_____
_____
_____
_____
_____
_____
_____
_____
_____
_____
_____
_____
_____
_____
_____
_____
_____
_____
_____
_____
_____

*Probe me, O God, and know my heart; try me and know my thoughts!*
*Psalm 139:23 NAB*

*You'll find when you smile*
*Your day will be brighter,*
*And all of your burdens*
*Will seem so much lighter.*

---

*I sought the Lord, and He answered me, and delivered me from all my fears. Look to him, and be radiant.*
*Psalm 34:4, 5*

*Faith is the key to heaven,*
*And only God's children hold*
*The key that opens the gateway*
*To that beautiful city of gold.*

_____
_____
_____
_____
_____
_____
_____
_____
_____
_____
_____
_____
_____
_____
_____
_____
_____
_____
_____
_____
_____
_____
_____
_____

**T**his is the gate of the Lord; the righteous shall enter through it.
*Psalm 118:20*

*True communication*
*Is reached through God alone,*
*To Him the thoughts we cannot express*
*Are understood and known.*

---

**H**ow precious to me are thy thoughts, O God!
*How vast is the sum of them!*
*Psalm 139:17*

"Love divine, all loves excelling"
Makes my humbled heart Your dwelling,
For without Your love divine
Total darkness would be mine.

_____

_____
_____
_____
_____
_____
_____
_____
_____
_____
_____
_____
_____
_____
_____
_____
_____
_____
_____
_____
_____
_____
_____
_____

*He who dwells in the shelter of the Most High, who abides in the shadow of the Almighty, will say to the Lord, "My refuge and my fortress ..."*
*Psalm 91:1 and 2*

*Faith is a force that is greater
Than knowledge or power or skill,
And the darkest defeat turns to triumph
If we trust in God's wisdom and will.*

_____

_____

_____

_____

_____

_____

_____

_____

_____

_____

_____

_____

_____

_____

_____

_____

_____

_____

_____

_____

_____

_____

*Trust in the Lord, and do good; so you will dwell in the land, and enjoy
security ... Commit your way to the Lord; trust in him, and he will act.*
*Psalm 37:3, 5*

Spring always comes with new life and birth
Followed by summer to warm the soft earth —
And what a comfort to know there are reasons
That souls, like nature, must have their seasons.

*He that goes forth weeping, bearing the seed for sowing, shall come home with shouts of joy, bringing his sheaves with him.*
*Psalm 126:6*

The nature of our attitude
Toward circumstantial things
Determines our acceptance
Of the problems that life brings.

*But I have calmed and quieted my soul, like a child quieted at
its mother's breast; like a child that is quieted is my soul.*
Psalm 131:2

*Love one another*
*And help those in need,*
*Regardless of colour,*
*Race, church, or creed.*

---

*Hatred stirs old quarrels, but love overlooks insults.*
*Proverbs 10:12 TLB*

So we may know God better
And feel His quiet power,
Let us daily keep in silence
A meditation hour.

_____
_____
_____
_____
_____
_____
_____
_____
_____
_____
_____
_____
_____
_____
_____
_____
_____
_____
_____
_____
_____
_____

*May the words of my mouth and the meditation of my heart
be pleasing in your sight, O Lord, my Rock and my Redeemer.*
*Psalm 19:15 NIV*

*A cheerful smile, a friendly word,*
*A sympathetic nod ...*
*These are all priceless treasures*
*From the storehouse of our God.*

_____
_____
_____
_____
_____
_____
_____
_____
_____
_____
_____
_____
_____
_____
_____
_____
_____
_____
_____
_____
_____
_____
_____
_____
_____

*To make an apt answer is a joy to a man,*
*and a word in season, how good it is!*
*Proverbs 15:23*

*I sometimes think that friendliness*
*Is like a cheerful song ...*
*It makes the good days better,*
*And it helps when things go wrong.*

The Lord is my strength and my shield; in him my heart trusts; so I am helped, and my heart exalts, and with my song I give thanks to him.
Psalm 28:7

Do not sit and idly wish for wider, new dimensions
Where you can put in practice all your good intentions,
But at the spot God placed you, begin at once to do
Little things to brighten up the lives surrounding you.

The path of the righteous is like the light of dawn,
which shines brighter and brighter until full day.
Proverbs 4:18

*Wait with a heart that is patient*
*For the goodness of God to prevail,*
*For never do our prayers go unanswered*
*And His mercy and love never fail.*

_____

_____

_____

_____

_____

_____

_____

_____

_____

_____

_____

_____

_____

_____

_____

_____

_____

_____

_____

_____

_____

_____

*Rest in the Lord and wait patiently for Him.*
*Psalm 37:7 NAS*

There's something we should not forget —
That people we've known or heard of or met
By indirection have a big part
In molding the thoughts of the mind and the heart.

_A_ man's heart deviseth his way:
but the Lord directeth his steps.
Proverbs 16:9 KJV

Among the great and glorious gifts
Our heavenly Father sends
Is the gift of understanding
That we find in loving friends.

_A_ friend loves at all times, and a brother is born for adversity.
Proverbs 17:17

*Great is your gladness*
*And rich your reward*
*When you make life's purpose*
*The choice of the Lord.*

_____

_____

_____

_____

_____

_____

_____

_____

_____

_____

_____

_____

_____

_____

_____

_____

_____

_____

_____

_____

_____

_____

_____

_____

_____

_____

*The reward for humility and fear of the*
*Lord is riches and honour and life.*
*Proverbs 22:4*

Happiness is something
We create in our mind,
It's something you search for
And so seldom find.

*Y*ou shall eat the fruit of the labour of your hands;
you shall be happy, and it shall be well with you.
*Psalm 128:2*

Every home
Is specially blessed
When God becomes
A daily guest.

_____

_____

_____

_____

_____

_____

_____

_____

_____

_____

_____

_____

_____

_____

_____

_____

_____

_____

_____

_____

_____

*Every day I will bless thee, and praise thy name for ever and ever.*
*Psalm 145:2*

May He who hears each little prayer
Keep you safely in His care
And make the world around you bright
As you walk daily in His light.

_____
_____
_____
_____
_____
_____
_____
_____
_____
_____
_____
_____
_____
_____
_____
_____
_____
_____
_____
_____
_____
_____
_____
_____

*Thy word is a lamp to my feet and a light to my path.*
Psalm 119:105

*No matter how big man's dreams are,*
*God's blessings are infinitely more,*
*For always God's giving is greater*
*Than what man is asking for.*

_____
_____
_____
_____
_____
_____
_____
_____
_____
_____
_____
_____
_____
_____
_____
_____
_____
_____
_____
_____
_____
_____
_____
_____

*He will receive blessing from the Lord, and*
*vindication from the God of his salvation.*
*Psalm 24:5*

*Dear God, what a comfort*
*To know that You care*
*And to know when I seek You,*
*You will always be there!*

_____
_____
_____
_____
_____
_____
_____
_____
_____
_____
_____
_____
_____
_____
_____
_____
_____
_____
_____
_____
_____
_____
_____
_____

*He keeps you from all evil, and preserves your life. He keeps his eye
upon you as you come and go, and always guards you.*
*Psalm 121:7, 8 TLB*

*Kneel in prayer in His presence,*
*And you'll find no need to speak.*
*For softly in silent communion,*
*God grants you the peace that you seek.*

_____
_____
_____
_____
_____
_____
_____
_____
_____
_____
_____
_____
_____
_____
_____
_____
_____
_____
_____
_____
_____
_____
_____
_____
_____
_____

*For God alone my soul waits in silence; from him comes my salvation.*
*Psalm 62:1*

*As you climb life's ladder,*
*Take faith along with you,*
*And great will be your happiness*
*As your dearest dreams come true.*

_____

_____
_____
_____
_____
_____
_____
_____
_____
_____
_____
_____
_____
_____
_____
_____
_____
_____
_____
_____
_____
_____
_____
_____
_____
_____
_____

*Love the Lord, all you his saints! The Lord preserves the*
*faithful, but abundantly requites him who acts haughtily.*
*Psalm 31:23*

*Grant me faith and courage,*
*Put purpose in my days,*
*Show me how to serve Thee*
*In the most effective ways.*

_____

_____

_____

_____

_____

_____

_____

_____

_____

_____

_____

_____

_____

_____

_____

_____

_____

_____

_____

_____

_____

_____

_____

_____

_____

_____

_____

*W*ait on the Lord: be of good courage, and he shall
strengthen thine heart: wait, I say, on the Lord.
*Psalm 27:14 KJV*

We are all God's children,
And He loves us — every one,
And completely forgives
All that we have done.

_____
_____
_____
_____
_____
_____
_____
_____
_____
_____
_____
_____
_____
_____
_____
_____
_____
_____
_____
_____
_____
_____
_____
_____

*Train up a child in the way he should go,
even when he is old he will not depart from it.
Proverbs 22:6 NAS*

*By completing what God*
*Gives us to do,*
*We find real contentment*
*And happiness, too.*

_____

_____

_____

_____

_____

_____

_____

_____

_____

_____

_____

_____

_____

_____

_____

_____

_____

_____

_____

_____

_____

*God blesses those who obey him; happy the*
*man who puts his trust in the Lord.*
*Proverbs 16:20 TLB*

To understand God's greatness
And to use His gifts each day
The soul must learn to meet Him
In a meditative way.

*To get wisdom is better than gold; to get
understanding is to be chosen rather than silver.*
Proverbs 16:16

We awaken in the morning,
Wondering how we'll meet the day,
Not knowing God stands ready
To help us if we pray.

_The integrity of the upright guides them, but the
crookedness of the treacherous destroys them._
Proverbs 11:3

The love of God surrounds us
Like the air we breathe around us –
As near as a heartbeat, as close as a prayer,
And whenever we need Him, He'll always be there.

_The Lord is faithful in all his words, and gracious in all his deeds._
Psalm 145:13

*Just like the seasons that come and go
When the flowers of spring lay buried in snow,
God sends to the heart in its winter of sadness
A springtime awakening of new hope and gladness.*

*And now, Lord, for what do I wait? My hope is in thee.*
*Psalm 39:7*

*Deal only with the present,*
*Never step into tomorrow,*
*For God asks us just to trust Him*
*And to never borrow sorrow.*

_____

_____

_____

_____

_____

_____

_____

_____

_____

_____

_____

_____

_____

_____

_____

_____

_____

_____

_____

*For our heart rejoices in Him, because we trust in His holy name.*
*Psalm 33:21 NAS*

When the door to our heart
Is open wide,
The sunshine of love
Will come inside.

_Probe me, O God, and know my heart; try me and know my thoughts!_
_Psalm 139:23 NAB_

*You'll find when you smile*
*Your day will be brighter,*
*And all of your burdens*
*Will seem so much lighter.*

---

*Faith is the key to heaven,*
*And only God's children hold*
*The key that opens the gateway*
*To that beautiful city of gold.*

_____

_____

_____

_____

_____

_____

_____

_____

_____

_____

_____

_____

_____

_____

_____

_____

_____

_____

_____

_____

_____

_____

_____

_____

_____

_____

*This is the gate of the Lord; the righteous shall enter through it.*
*Psalm 118:20*

True communication
Is reached through God alone,
To Him the thoughts we cannot express
Are understood and known.

_____
_____
_____
_____
_____
_____
_____
_____
_____
_____
_____
_____
_____
_____
_____
_____
_____
_____
_____
_____
_____
_____
_____
_____
_____
_____
_____

*How* precious to me are thy thoughts, O God!
*How vast is the sum of them!*
*Psalm 139:17*

*"Love divine, all loves excelling"*
*Makes my humbled heart Your dwelling,*
*For without Your love divine*
*Total darkness would be mine.*

_____

_____
_____
_____
_____
_____
_____
_____
_____
_____
_____
_____
_____
_____
_____
_____
_____
_____
_____
_____
_____
_____
_____
_____
_____
_____

*He who dwells in the shelter of the Most High, who abides in the sha-*
*dow of the Almighty, will say to the Lord, "My refuge and my fortress ..."*
*Psalm 91:1 and 2*

Faith is a force that is greater
Than knowledge or power or skill,
And the darkest defeat turns to triumph
If we trust in God's wisdom and will.

_____

_____

_____

_____

_____

_____

_____

_____

_____

_____

_____

_____

_____

_____

_____

_____

_____

_____

_____

_____

_____

_____

*Trust in the Lord, and do good; so you will dwell in the land, and enjoy security ... Commit your way to the Lord; trust in him, and he will act.*
Psalm 37:3, 5

*Spring always comes with new life and birth*
*Followed by summer to warm the soft earth —*
*And what a comfort to know there are reasons*
*That souls, like nature, must have their seasons.*

_____

_____
_____
_____
_____
_____
_____
_____
_____
_____
_____
_____
_____
_____
_____
_____
_____
_____
_____
_____
_____
_____
_____
_____

*He that goes forth weeping, bearing the seed for sowing, shall come*
*home with shouts of joy, bringing his sheaves with him.*
*Psalm 126:6*

*The nature of our attitude*
*Toward circumstantial things*
*Determines our acceptance*
*Of the problems that life brings.*

_____

_____

_____

_____

_____

_____

_____

_____

_____

_____

_____

_____

_____

_____

_____

_____

_____

_____

_____

_____

_____

_____

_____

_____

_____

_____

_____

*But I have calmed and quieted my soul, like a child quieted at its mother's breast; like a child that is quieted is my soul.*
*Psalm 131:2*

*Love one another*
*And help those in need,*
*Regardless of colour,*
*Race, church, or creed.*

---

*Hatred stirs old quarrels, but love overlooks insults.*
*Proverbs 10:12 TLB*

So we may know God better
And feel His quiet power,
Let us daily keep in silence
A meditation hour.

_____

_____

_____

_____

_____

_____

_____

_____

_____

_____

_____

_____

_____

_____

_____

_____

_____

_____

_____

_____

_____

_____

_____

_____

_____

*May the words of my mouth and the meditation of my heart*
*be pleasing in your sight, O Lord, my Rock and my Redeemer.*
*Psalm 19:15 NIV*

*A cheerful smile, a friendly word,*
*A sympathetic nod ...*
*These are all priceless treasures*
*From the storehouse of our God.*

*To make an apt answer is a joy to a man,*
*and a word in season, how good it is!*
*Proverbs 15:23*

*I sometimes think that friendliness*
*Is like a cheerful song ...*
*It makes the good days better,*
*And it helps when things go wrong.*

---

*The Lord is my strength and my shield; in him my heart trusts; so I am helped, and my heart exalts, and with my song I give thanks to him.*
*Psalm 28:7*

*Do not sit and idly wish for wider, new dimensions*
*Where you can put in practice all your good intentions,*
*But at the spot God placed you, begin at once to do*
*Little things to brighten up the lives surrounding you.*

---

*The path of the righteous is like the light of dawn,*
*which shines brighter and brighter until full day.*
Proverbs 4:18

*Wait with a heart that is patient*
*For the goodness of God to prevail,*
*For never do our prayers go unanswered*
*And His mercy and love never fail.*

---

*Rest in the Lord and wait patiently for Him.*
*Psalm 37:7 NAS*

There's something we should not forget —
That people we've known or heard of or met
By indirection have a big part
In molding the thoughts of the mind and the heart.

*A* man's heart deviseth his way:
but the Lord directeth his steps.
*Proverbs 16:9 KJV*

*Among the great and glorious gifts*
*Our heavenly Father sends*
*Is the gift of understanding*
*That we find in loving friends.*

*A friend loves at all times, and a brother is born for adversity.*
*Proverbs 17:17*

*Great is your gladness*
*And rich your reward*
*When you make life's purpose*
*The choice of the Lord.*

---

*The reward for humility and fear of the*
*Lord is riches and honour and life.*
*Proverbs 22:4*

Happiness is something
We create in our mind,
It's something you search for
And so seldom find.

_____

_____

_____

_____

_____

_____

_____

_____

_____

_____

_____

_____

_____

_____

_____

_____

_____

_____

_____

_____

_____

_____

_____

_____

_____

_____

*You shall eat the fruit of the labour of your hands;*
*you shall be happy, and it shall be well with you.*
*Psalm 128:2*

*Every home*
*Is specially blessed*
*When God becomes*
*A daily guest.*

_____

_____

_____

_____

_____

_____

_____

_____

_____

_____

_____

_____

_____

_____

_____

_____

_____

_____

_____

_____

_____

_____

_____

*Every day I will bless thee, and praise thy name for ever and ever.*
*Psalm 145:2*

May He who hears each little prayer
Keep you safely in His care
And make the world around you bright
As you walk daily in His light.

_____

Thy word is a lamp to my feet and a light to my path.
Psalm 119:105

*No matter how big man's dreams are,*
*God's blessings are infinitely more,*
*For always God's giving is greater*
*Than what man is asking for.*

_____
_____
_____
_____
_____
_____
_____
_____
_____
_____
_____
_____
_____
_____
_____
_____
_____
_____
_____
_____
_____
_____
_____
_____

*He will receive blessing from the Lord, and*
*vindication from the God of his salvation.*
*Psalm 24:5*

Dear God, what a comfort
To know that You care
And to know when I seek You,
You will always be there!

_____

_____
_____
_____
_____
_____
_____
_____
_____
_____
_____
_____
_____
_____
_____
_____
_____
_____
_____
_____
_____
_____
_____
_____
_____

*He keeps you from all evil, and preserves your life. He keeps his eye
upon you as you come and go, and always guards you.
Psalm 121:7, 8 TLB*

*Kneel in prayer in His presence,*
*And you'll find no need to speak.*
*For softly  in silent communion,*
*God grants you the peace that you seek.*

_____

_____
_____
_____
_____
_____
_____
_____
_____
_____
_____
_____
_____
_____
_____
_____
_____
_____
_____
_____
_____
_____
_____

*For God alone my soul waits in silence; from him comes my salvation.*
*Psalm 62:1*

*As you climb life's ladder,*
*Take faith along with you,*
*And great will be your happiness*
*As your dearest dreams come true.*

_____
_____
_____
_____
_____
_____
_____
_____
_____
_____
_____
_____
_____
_____
_____
_____
_____
_____
_____
_____
_____
_____
_____
_____
_____
_____

*Love the Lord, all you his saints! The Lord preserves the*
*faithful, but abundantly requites him who acts haughtily.*
*Psalm 31:23*

*Grant me faith and courage,*
*Put purpose in my days,*
*Show me how to serve Thee*
*In the most effective ways.*

*Wait on the Lord: be of good courage, and he shall*
*strengthen thine heart: wait, I say, on the Lord.*
*Psalm 27:14 KJV*

We are all God's children,
And He loves us — every one,
And completely forgives
All that we have done.

_____

_____

_____

_____

_____

_____

_____

_____

_____

_____

_____

_____

_____

_____

_____

_____

_____

_____

_____

_____

_____

_____

_____

*Train up a child in the way he should go,
even when he is old he will not depart from it.
Proverbs 22:6 NAS*

*By completing what God*
*Gives us to do,*
*We find real contentment*
*And happiness, too.*

_____

_____

_____

_____

_____

_____

_____

_____

_____

_____

_____

_____

_____

_____

_____

_____

_____

_____

_____

_____

_____

_____

_____

_____

_____

*God blesses those who obey him; happy the*
*man who puts his trust in the Lord.*
*Proverbs 16:20 TLB*

To understand God's greatness
And to use His gifts each day
The soul must learn to meet Him
In a meditative way.

---

*To* get wisdom is better than gold; to get
understanding is to be chosen rather than silver.
Proverbs 16:16

*We awaken in the morning,*
*Wondering how we'll meet the day,*
*Not knowing God stands ready*
*To help us if we pray.*

_____

_____

_____

_____

_____

_____

_____

_____

_____

_____

_____

_____

_____

_____

_____

_____

_____

_____

_____

_____

_____

_____

_____

_____

_____

*The integrity of the upright guides them, but the*
*crookedness of the treacherous destroys them.*
*Proverbs 11:3*

The love of God surrounds us
Like the air we breathe around us —
As near as a heartbeat, as close as a prayer,
And whenever we need Him, He'll always be there.

_____
_____
_____
_____
_____
_____
_____
_____
_____
_____
_____
_____
_____
_____
_____
_____
_____
_____
_____
_____
_____
_____
_____

*The Lord is faithful in all his words, and gracious in all his deeds.*
*Psalm 145:13*

*Just like the seasons that come and go*
*When the flowers of spring lay buried in snow,*
*God sends to the heart in its winter of sadness*
*A springtime awakening of new hope and gladness.*

*And now, Lord, for what do I wait? My hope is in thee.*
*Psalm 39:7*

*Deal only with the present,*
*Never step into tomorrow,*
*For God asks us just to trust Him*
*And to never borrow sorrow.*

*For our heart rejoices in Him, because we trust in His holy name.*
*Psalm 33:21 NAS*

*When the door to our heart*
*Is open wide,*
*The sunshine of love*
*Will come inside.*

_____

_____

_____

_____

_____

_____

_____

_____

_____

_____

_____

_____

_____

_____

_____

_____

_____

_____

_____

_____

_____

_____

_____

_____

_____

_____

_____

_____

*Probe me, O God, and know my heart; try me and know my thoughts!*
*Psalm 139:23 NAB*

*You'll find when you smile*
*Your day will be brighter,*
*And all of your burdens*
*Will seem so much lighter.*

_____
_____
_____
_____
_____
_____
_____
_____
_____
_____
_____
_____
_____
_____
_____
_____
_____
_____
_____
_____
_____
_____

*I sought the Lord, and He answered me, and delivered*
*me from all my fears. Look to him, and be radiant.*
*Psalm 34:4, 5*

*Faith is the key to heaven,*
*And only God's children hold*
*The key that opens the gateway*
*To that beautiful city of gold.*

_____
_____
_____
_____
_____
_____
_____
_____
_____
_____
_____
_____
_____
_____
_____
_____
_____
_____
_____
_____
_____
_____
_____

*This is the gate of the Lord; the righteous shall enter through it.*
*Psalm 118:20*

True communication
Is reached through God alone,
To Him the thoughts we cannot express
Are understood and known.

_____
_____
_____
_____
_____
_____
_____
_____
_____
_____
_____
_____
_____
_____
_____
_____
_____
_____
_____
_____
_____
_____
_____
_____

*How precious to me are thy thoughts, O God!*
*How vast is the sum of them!*
*Psalm 139:17*

"Love divine, all loves excelling"
Makes my humbled heart Your dwelling,
For without Your love divine
Total darkness would be mine.

_____

_____

_____

_____

_____

_____

_____

_____

_____

_____

_____

_____

_____

_____

_____

_____

_____

_____

_____

_____

_____

_____

_____

_____

*He who dwells in the shelter of the Most High, who abides in the shadow of the Almighty, will say to the Lord, "My refuge and my fortress ..."*
*Psalm 91:1 and 2*

Faith is a force that is greater
Than knowledge or power or skill,
And the darkest defeat turns to triumph
If we trust in God's wisdom and will.

_____
_____
_____
_____
_____
_____
_____
_____
_____
_____
_____
_____
_____
_____
_____
_____
_____
_____
_____
_____
_____

*Trust in the Lord, and do good; so you will dwell in the land, and enjoy security ... Commit your way to the Lord; trust in him, and he will act.*
Psalm 37:3, 5

*Spring always comes with new life and birth*
*Followed by summer to warm the soft earth —*
*And what a comfort to know there are reasons*
*That souls, like nature, must have their seasons.*

_____

_____

_____

_____

_____

_____

_____

_____

_____

_____

_____

_____

_____

_____

_____

_____

_____

_____

_____

_____

_____

*He that goes forth weeping, bearing the seed for sowing, shall come*
*home with shouts of joy, bringing his sheaves with him.*
*Psalm 126:6*

The nature of our attitude
Toward circumstantial things
Determines our acceptance
Of the problems that life brings.

_____

_____

_____

_____

_____

_____

_____

_____

_____

_____

_____

_____

_____

_____

_____

_____

_____

_____

_____

_____

_____

_____

_____

_____

_____

_____

*But I have calmed and quieted my soul, like a child quieted at
its mother's breast; like a child that is quieted is my soul.
Psalm 131:2*

*Love one another
And help those in need,
Regardless of colour,
Race, church, or creed.*

_____
_____
_____
_____
_____
_____
_____
_____
_____
_____
_____
_____
_____
_____
_____
_____
_____
_____
_____
_____
_____
_____
_____
_____
_____
_____
_____

*Hatred stirs old quarrels, but love overlooks insults.*
*Proverbs 10:12 TLB*

So we may know God better
And feel His quiet power,
Let us daily keep in silence
A meditation hour.

_____

_____

_____

_____

_____

_____

_____

_____

_____

_____

_____

_____

_____

_____

_____

_____

_____

_____

_____

_____

_____

_____

_____

_____

_____

_____

*May the words of my mouth and the meditation of my heart
be pleasing in your sight, O Lord, my Rock and my Redeemer.
Psalm 19:15 NIV*

*A cheerful smile, a friendly word,*
*A sympathetic nod ...*
*These are all priceless treasures*
*From the storehouse of our God.*

*T*o make an apt answer is a joy to a man,
and a word in season, how good it is!
Proverbs 15:23

*I sometimes think that friendliness*
*Is like a cheerful song …*
*It makes the good days better,*
*And it helps when things go wrong.*

_____

_____

_____

_____

_____

_____

_____

_____

_____

_____

_____

_____

_____

_____

_____

_____

_____

_____

_____

_____

_____

_____

*The Lord is my strength and my shield; in him my heart trusts; so I am helped, and my heart exalts, and with my song I give thanks to him.*
*Psalm 28:7*

*Do not sit and idly wish for wider, new dimensions*
*Where you can put in practice all your good intentions,*
*But at the spot God placed you, begin at once to do*
*Little things to brighten up the lives surrounding you.*

---

*The path of the righteous is like the light of dawn,*
*which shines brighter and brighter until full day.*
Proverbs 4:18

*Wait with a heart that is patient*
*For the goodness of God to prevail,*
*For never do our prayers go unanswered*
*And His mercy and love never fail.*

*Rest in the Lord and wait patiently for Him.*
*Psalm 37:7 NAS*

There's something we should not forget —
That people we've known or heard of or met
By indirection have a big part
In molding the thoughts of the mind and the heart.

*A* man's heart deviseth his way:
but the Lord directeth his steps.
Proverbs 16:9 KJV

*Among the great and glorious gifts*
*Our heavenly Father sends*
*Is the gift of understanding*
*That we find in loving friends.*

*A friend loves at all times, and a brother is born for adversity.*
*Proverbs 17:17*

*Great is your gladness*
*And rich your reward*
*When you make life's purpose*
*The choice of the Lord.*

_____

---

***T**he reward for humility and fear of the*
*Lord is riches and honour and life.*
*Proverbs 22:4*

Happiness is something
We create in our mind,
It's something you search for
And so seldom find.

_____

_____

_____

_____

_____

_____

_____

_____

_____

_____

_____

_____

_____

_____

_____

_____

_____

_____

_____

_____

_____

_____

*You shall eat the fruit of the labour of your hands;*
*you shall be happy, and it shall be well with you.*
*Psalm 128:2*

*Every home*
*Is specially blessed*
*When God becomes*
*A daily guest.*

_____

_____

_____

_____

_____

_____

_____

_____

_____

_____

_____

_____

_____

_____

_____

_____

_____

_____

_____

_____

_____

_____

_____

*Every day I will bless thee, and praise thy name for ever and ever.*
*Psalm 145:2*

May He who hears each little prayer
Keep you safely in His care
And make the world around you bright
As you walk daily in His light.

_Thy word is a lamp to my feet and a light to my path._
Psalm 119:105

*No matter how big man's dreams are,*
*God's blessings are infinitely more,*
*For always God's giving is greater*
*Than what man is asking for.*

*He will receive blessing from the Lord, and*
*vindication from the God of his salvation.*
Psalm 24:5

Dear God, what a comfort
To know that You care
And to know when I seek You,
You will always be there!

_____
_____
_____
_____
_____
_____
_____
_____
_____
_____
_____
_____
_____
_____
_____
_____
_____
_____
_____
_____
_____
_____
_____
_____
_____
_____
_____
_____

*He keeps you from all evil, and preserves your life. He keeps his eye
upon you as you come and go, and always guards you.*
*Psalm 121:7, 8 TLB*

*Kneel in prayer in His presence,*
*And you'll find no need to speak.*
*For softly  in silent communion,*
*God grants you the peace that you seek.*

_____

_____
_____
_____
_____
_____
_____
_____
_____
_____
_____
_____
_____
_____
_____
_____
_____
_____
_____
_____
_____
_____
_____
_____
_____

*For God alone my soul waits in silence; from him comes my salvation.*
*Psalm 62:1*

As you climb life's ladder,
Take faith along with you,
And great will be your happiness
As your dearest dreams come true.

_Love the Lord, all you his saints! The Lord preserves the
faithful, but abundantly requites him who acts haughtily._
Psalm 31:23

Grant me faith and courage,
Put purpose in my days,
Show me how to serve Thee
In the most effective ways.

_____

_____

_____

_____

_____

_____

_____

_____

_____

_____

_____

_____

_____

_____

_____

_____

_____

_____

_____

_____

_____

_____

_____

Wait on the Lord: be of good courage, and he shall
strengthen thine heart: wait, I say, on the Lord.
Psalm 27:14 KJV

We are all God's children,
And He loves us — every one,
And completely forgives
All that we have done.

*T*rain up a child in the way he should go,
even when he is old he will not depart from it.
*Proverbs 22:6 NAS*

By completing what God
Gives us to do,
We find real contentment
And happiness, too.

*God blesses those who obey him; happy the
man who puts his trust in the Lord.*
Proverbs 16:20 TLB

*To understand God's greatness*
*And to use His gifts each day*
*The soul must learn to meet Him*
*In a meditative way.*

**T**o get wisdom is better than gold; to get
understanding is to be chosen rather than silver.
*Proverbs 16:16*

*We awaken in the morning,*
*Wondering how we'll meet the day,*
*Not knowing God stands ready*
*To help us if we pray.*

_____

The integrity of the upright guides them, but the
crookedness of the treacherous destroys them.
*Proverbs 11:3*

The love of God surrounds us
Like the air we breathe around us —
As near as a heartbeat, as close as a prayer,
And whenever we need Him, He'll always be there.

_____

_____

_____

_____

_____

_____

_____

_____

_____

_____

_____

_____

_____

_____

_____

_____

_____

_____

_____

_____

_____

*The Lord is faithful in all his words, and gracious in all his deeds.*
*Psalm 145:13*

*Just like the seasons that come and go*
*When the flowers of spring lay buried in snow,*
*God sends to the heart in its winter of sadness*
*A springtime awakening of new hope and gladness.*

*And now, Lord, for what do I wait? My hope is in thee.*
*Psalm 39:7*

Deal only with the present,
Never step into tomorrow,
For God asks us just to trust Him
And to never borrow sorrow.

*For our heart rejoices in Him, because we trust in His holy name.*
*Psalm 33:21 NAS*

When the door to our heart
Is open wide,
The sunshine of love
Will come inside.

*Probe me, O God, and know my heart; try me and know my thoughts!*
*Psalm 139:23 NAB*

*You'll find when you smile*
*Your day will be brighter,*
*And all of your burdens*
*Will seem so much lighter.*

---

*I sought the Lord, and He answered me, and delivered
me from all my fears. Look to him, and be radiant.*
Psalm 34:4, 5

*Faith is the key to heaven,*
*And only God's children hold*
*The key that opens the gateway*
*To that beautiful city of gold.*

_____

**T**his is the gate of the Lord; the righteous shall enter through it.
Psalm 118:20

*True communication*
*Is reached through God alone,*
*To Him the thoughts we cannot express*
*Are understood and known.*

_____

_____
_____
_____
_____
_____
_____
_____
_____
_____
_____
_____
_____
_____
_____
_____
_____
_____
_____
_____
_____
_____
_____
_____
_____
_____
_____

*How precious to me are thy thoughts, O God!*
*How vast is the sum of them!*
*Psalm 139:17*

"Love divine, all loves excelling"
Makes my humbled heart Your dwelling,
For without Your love divine
Total darkness would be mine.

He who dwells in the shelter of the Most High, who abides in the shadow of the Almighty, will say to the Lord, "My refuge and my fortress ..."
Psalm 91:1 and 2

Faith is a force that is greater
Than knowledge or power or skill,
And the darkest defeat turns to triumph
If we trust in God's wisdom and will.

_____
_____
_____
_____
_____
_____
_____
_____
_____
_____
_____
_____
_____
_____
_____
_____
_____
_____
_____
_____
_____
_____
_____

*Trust in the Lord, and do good; so you will dwell in the land, and enjoy
security ... Commit your way to the Lord; trust in him, and he will act.*
*Psalm 37:3, 5*

Spring always comes with new life and birth
Followed by summer to warm the soft earth —
And what a comfort to know there are reasons
That souls, like nature, must have their seasons.

He that goes forth weeping, bearing the seed for sowing, shall come
home with shouts of joy, bringing his sheaves with him.
Psalm 126:6

The nature of our attitude
Toward circumstantial things
Determines our acceptance
Of the problems that life brings.

_____

_____

_____

_____

_____

_____

_____

_____

_____

_____

_____

_____

_____

_____

_____

_____

_____

_____

_____

_____

_____

_____

_____

_____

_____

_____

*But I have calmed and quieted my soul, like a child quieted at*
*its mother's breast; like a child that is quieted is my soul.*
*Psalm 131:2*

*Love one another
And help those in need,
Regardless of colour,
Race, church, or creed.*

_____
_____
_____
_____
_____
_____
_____
_____
_____
_____
_____
_____
_____
_____
_____
_____
_____
_____
_____
_____
_____
_____
_____
_____
_____
_____

*Hatred stirs old quarrels, but love overlooks insults.
Proverbs 10:12 TLB*